Robert Pace

FINGER BUILDERS

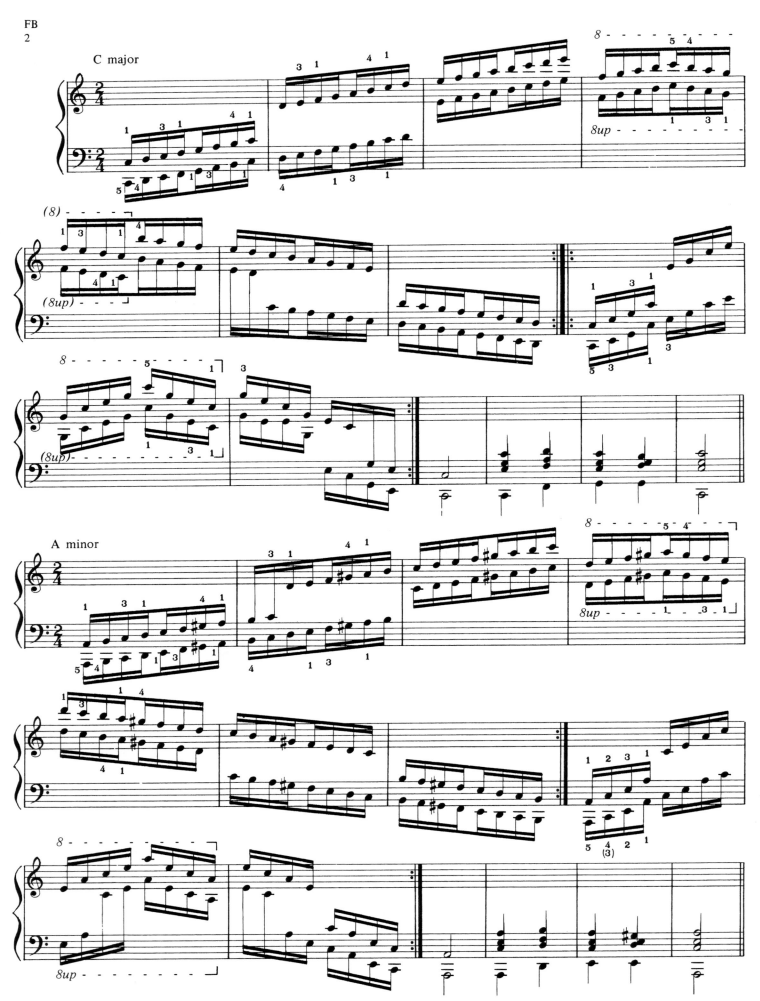

Transpose to G major and E minor.

Transpose to a different key each day beginning with G major (G, D, A, E and B major)

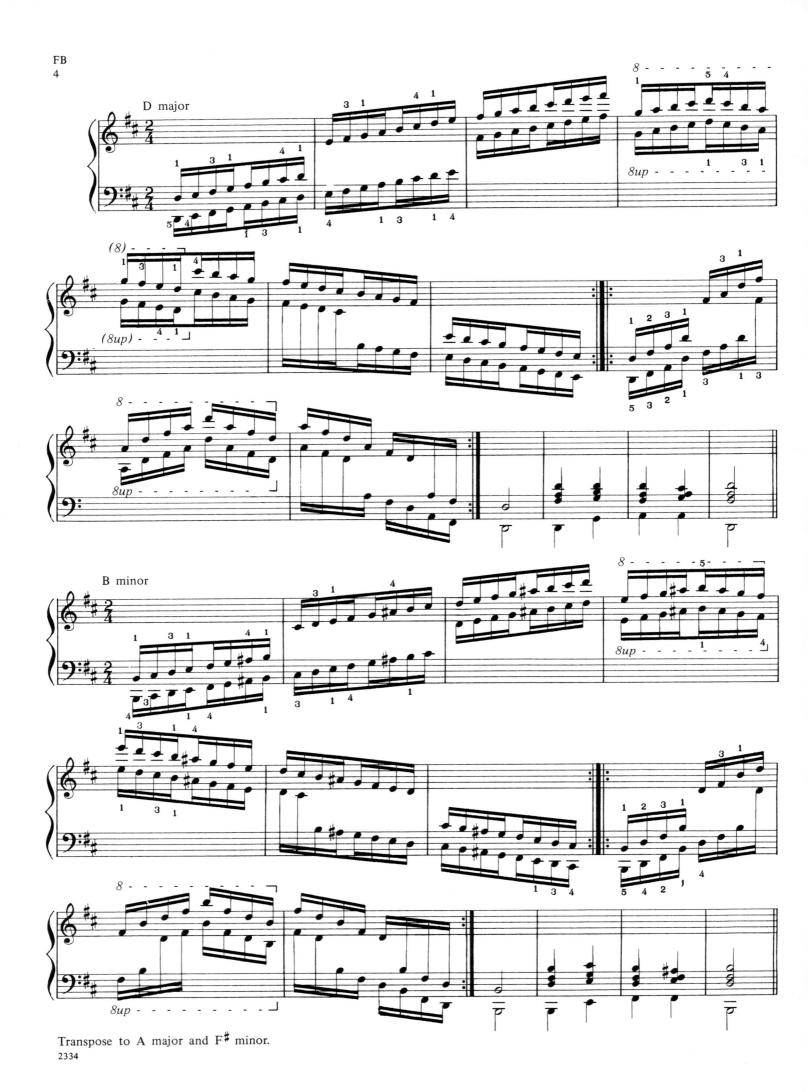

Transpose to A major and F# minor.

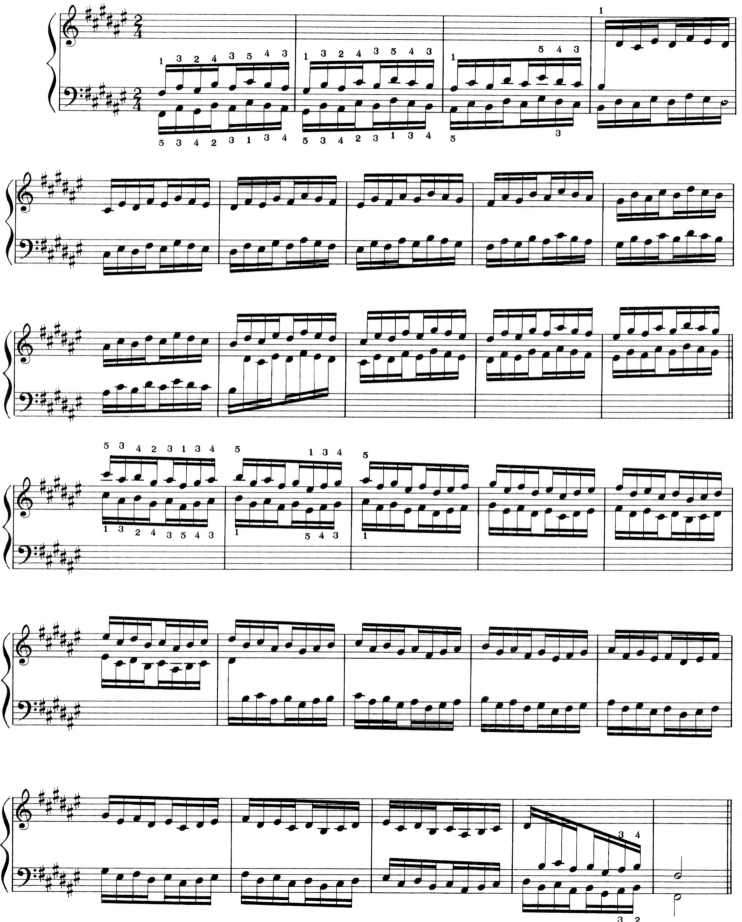

Each day play a different one of the keys shown here: D♭, A♭, E♭, B♭ and F major.

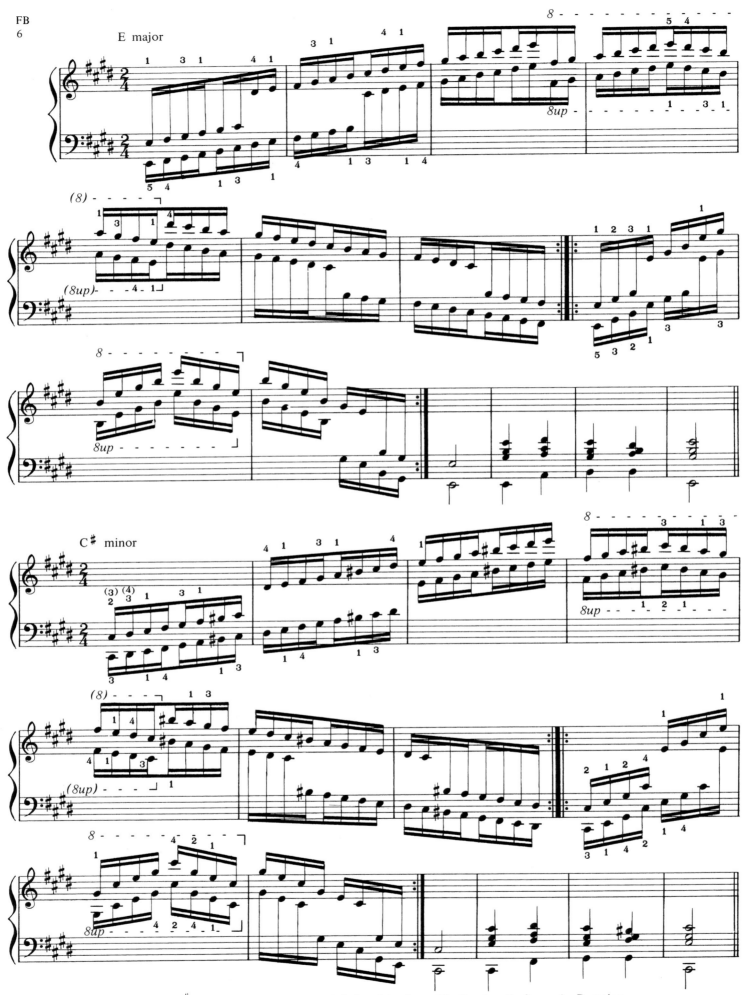

Transpose to B major and G# minor. Notice that the left hand begins with the fourth finger in B major.

Play as written the first day, then the second day go down by half steps to B, B♭, A, etc.
Continue to alternate up and down on succeeding days.

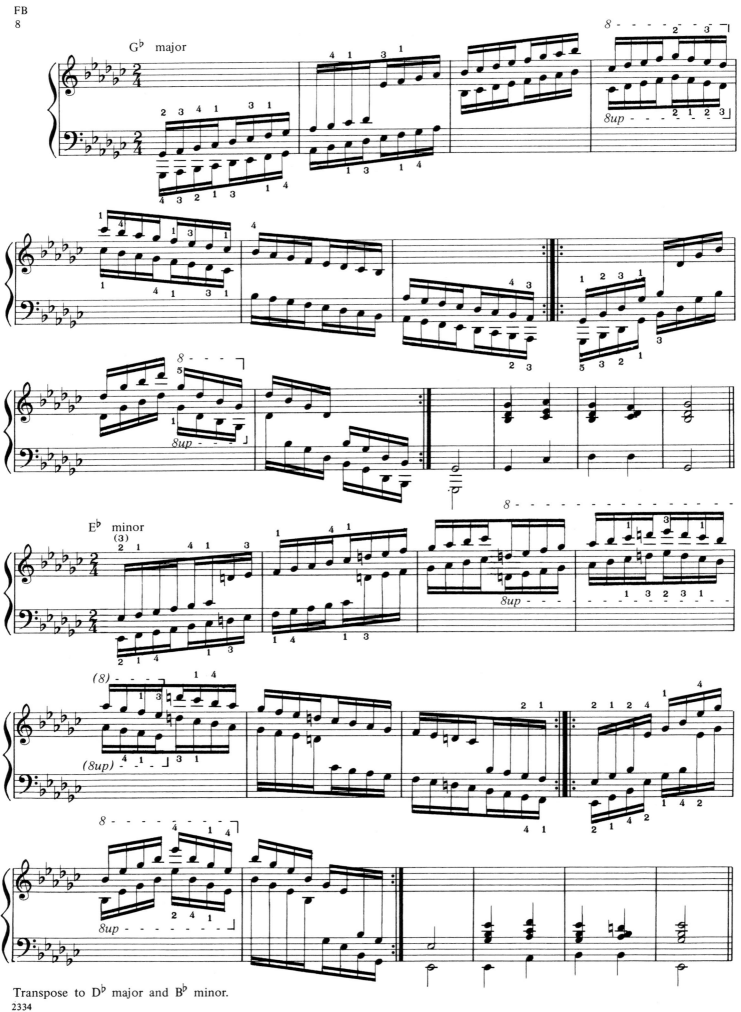

Transpose to D♭ major and B♭ minor.

Play as written, then each day select a different key from this group: G, D, A, E, and B major.

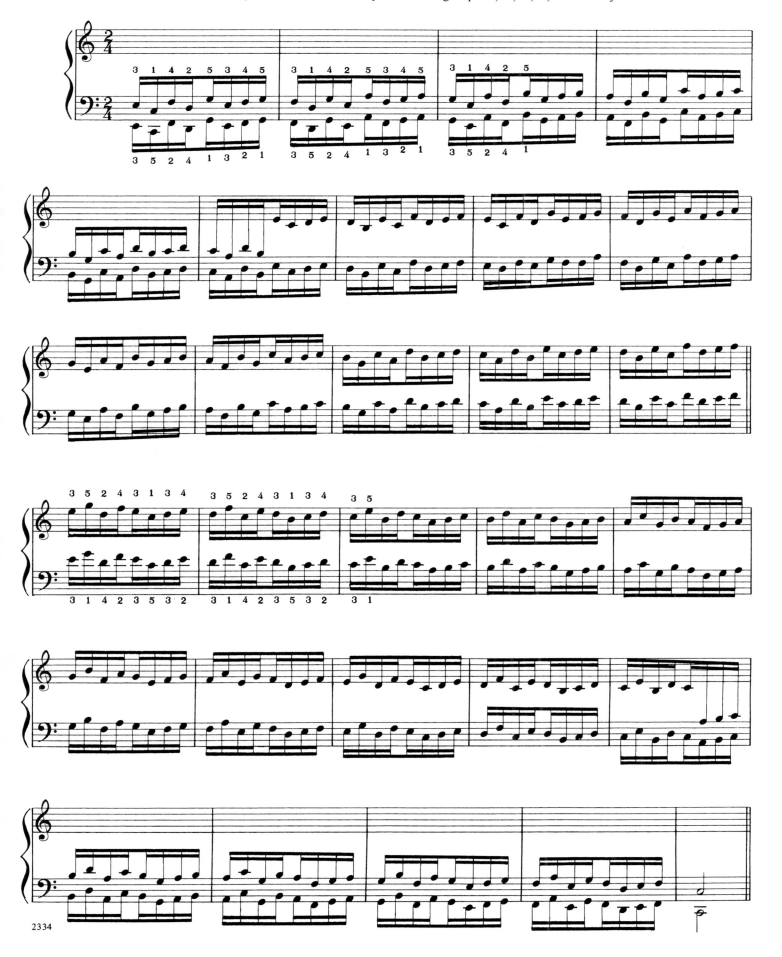

2334

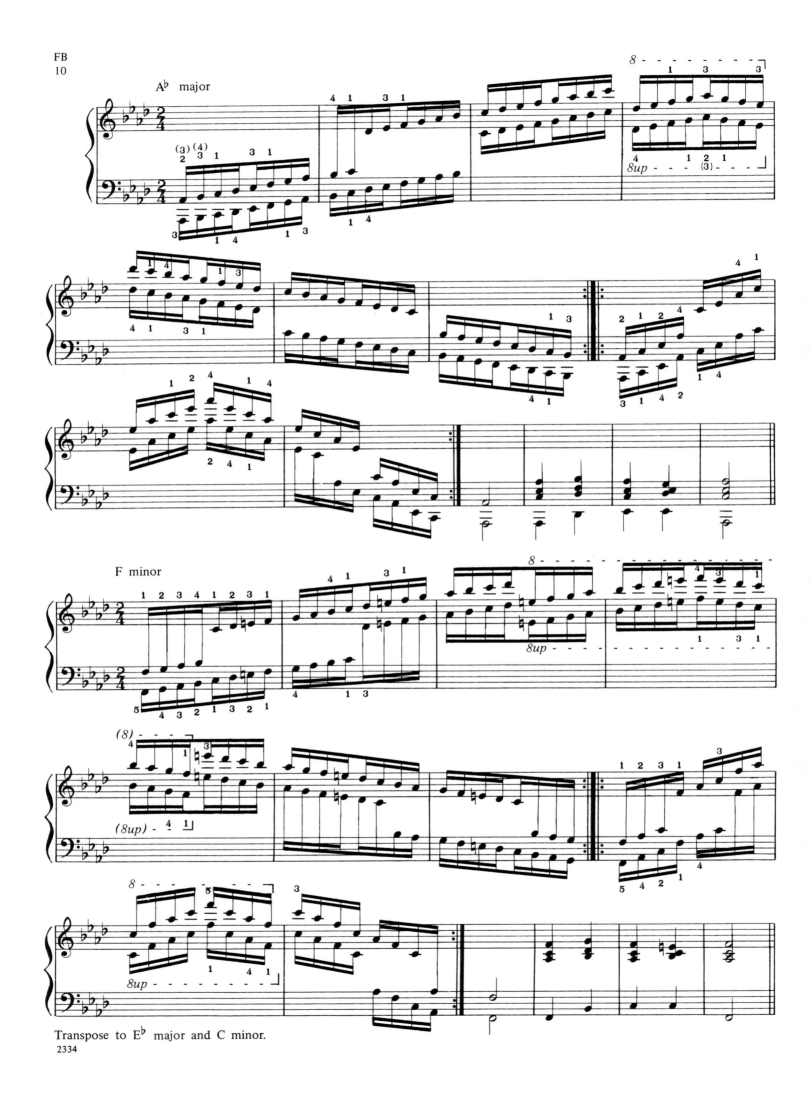

Transpose to E♭ major and C minor.

Transpose daily to a different key as shown here: D♭, A♭, E♭, B♭, and F major.

Transpose to F major and D minor.

In addition to practicing this in various rhythms and with different dynamics, play it going down the chromatic scale from C.

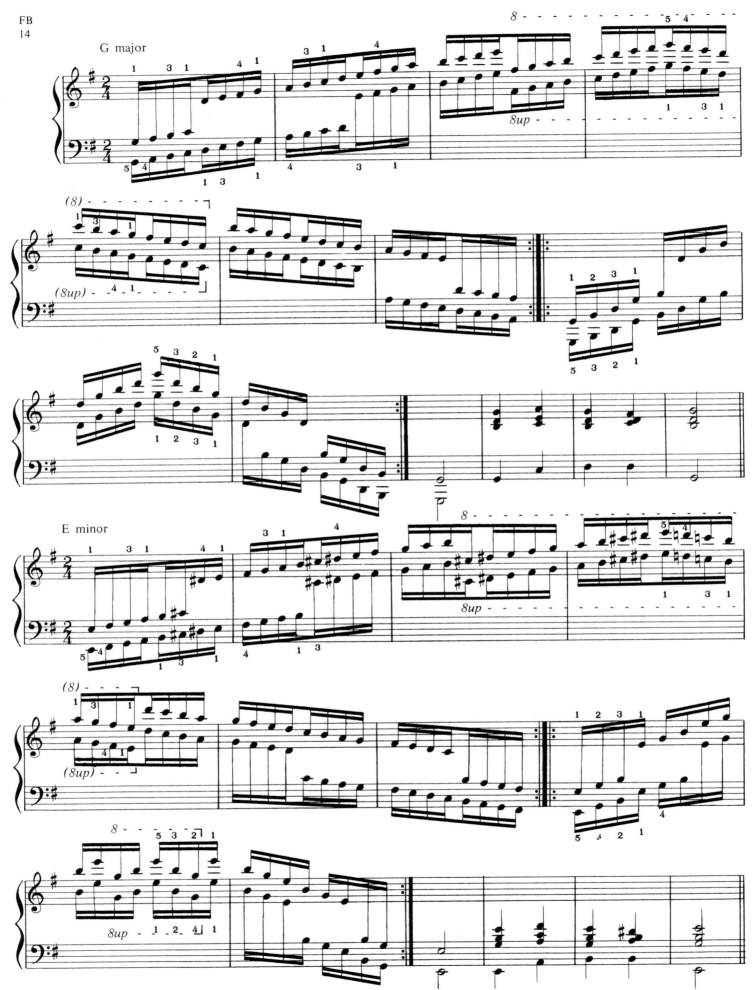

Notice the use of melodic minor in the ascending scale, and the natural minor descending.
Transpose to D major and B minor.

The first day play in the key of C major, then each day transpose up one-half step to a new key (D♭, D, E♭, and F major).

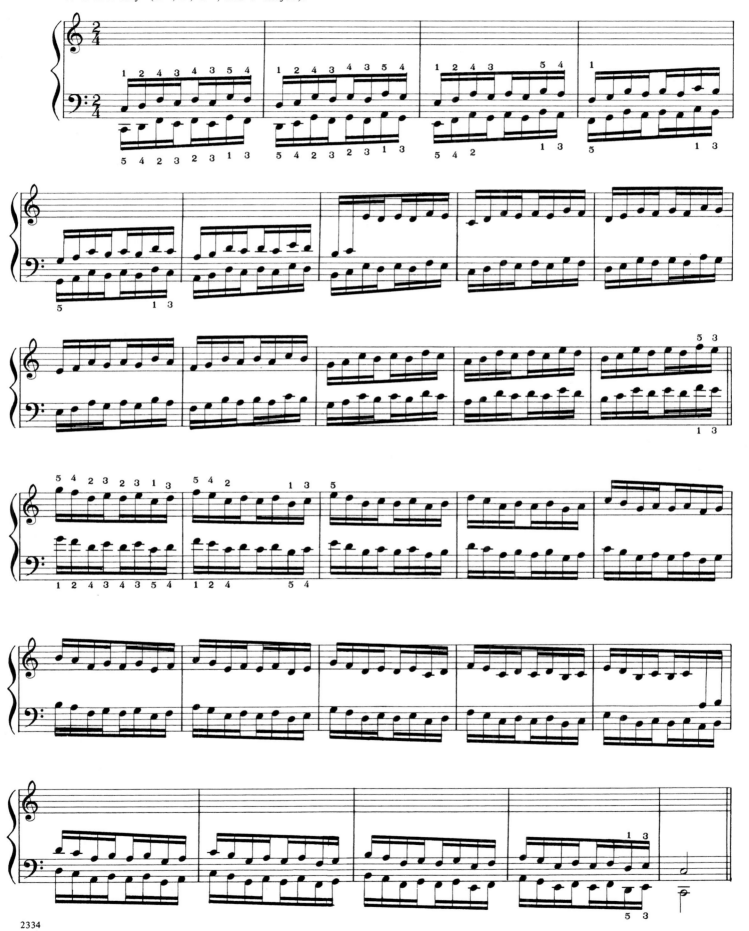

2334

A major

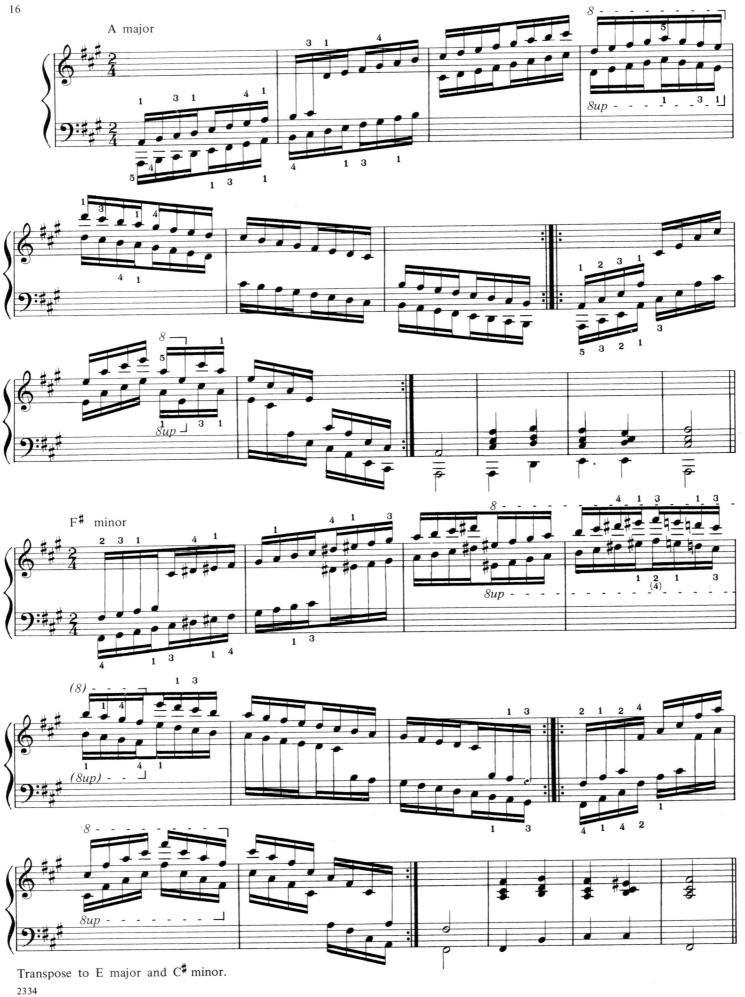

F# minor

Transpose to E major and C# minor.

Play first in G major as written, then each day transpose up one–half step
to these keys: G, A♭, A, B♭ and B major.

B major

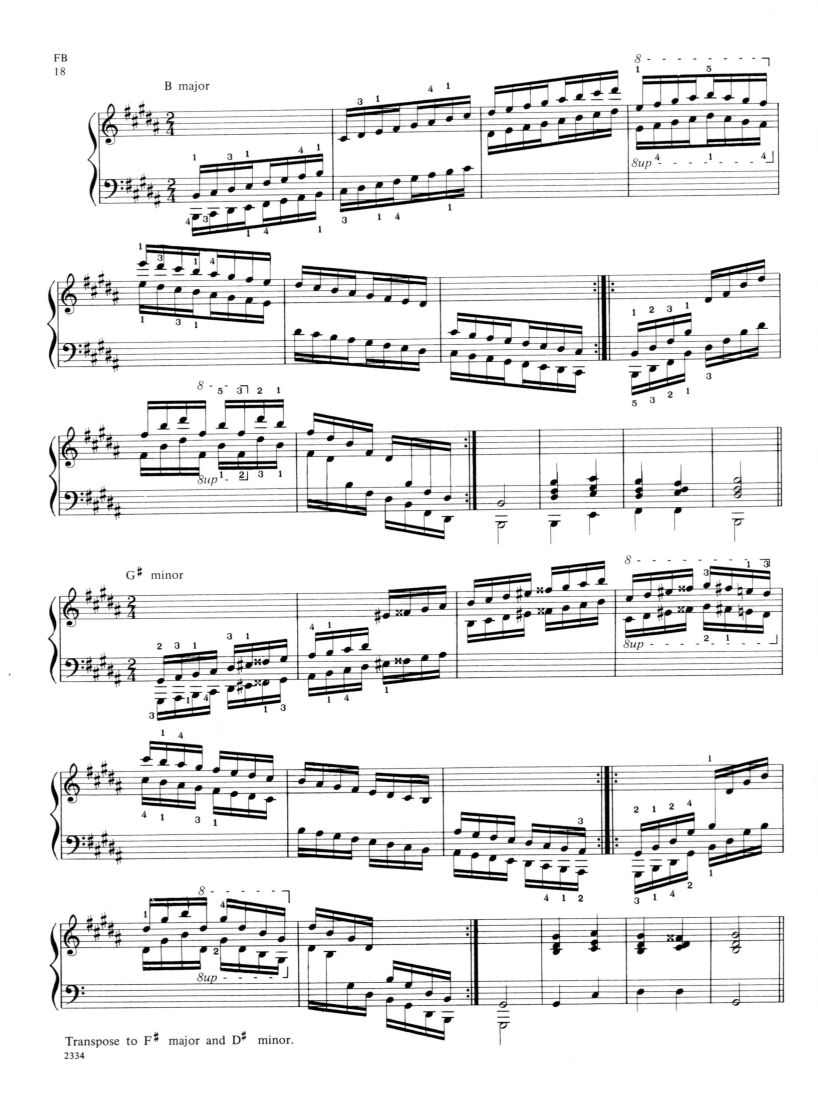

G# minor

Transpose to F# major and D# minor.

Use a very legato touch with firm fingers (no bouncing of the wrists).

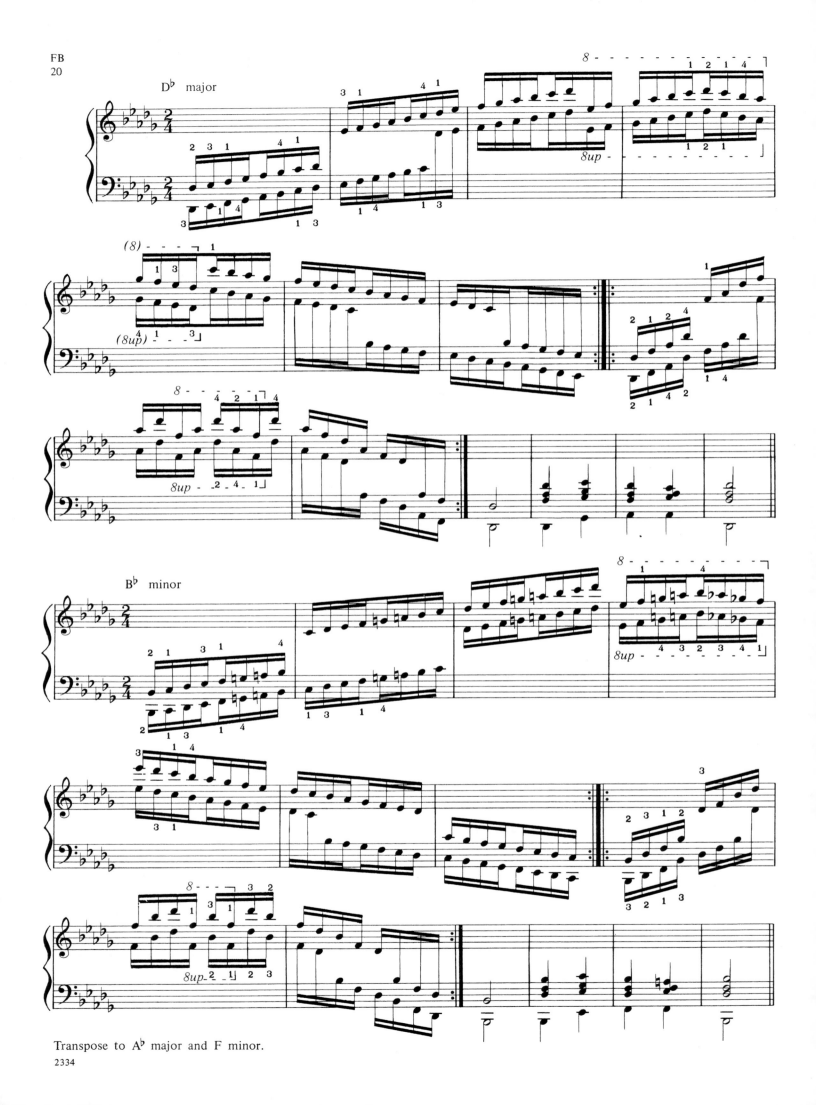

Transpose to A♭ major and F minor.

Each day transpose down to another key (B, B$^\flat$, A, A$^\flat$, and G major).

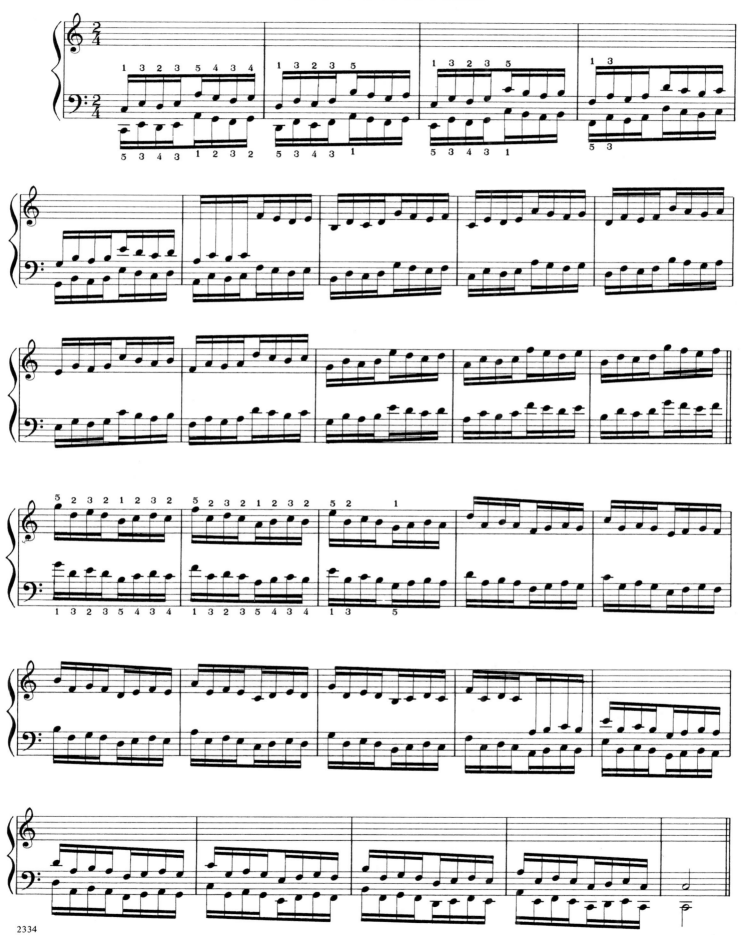

2334

E♭ major

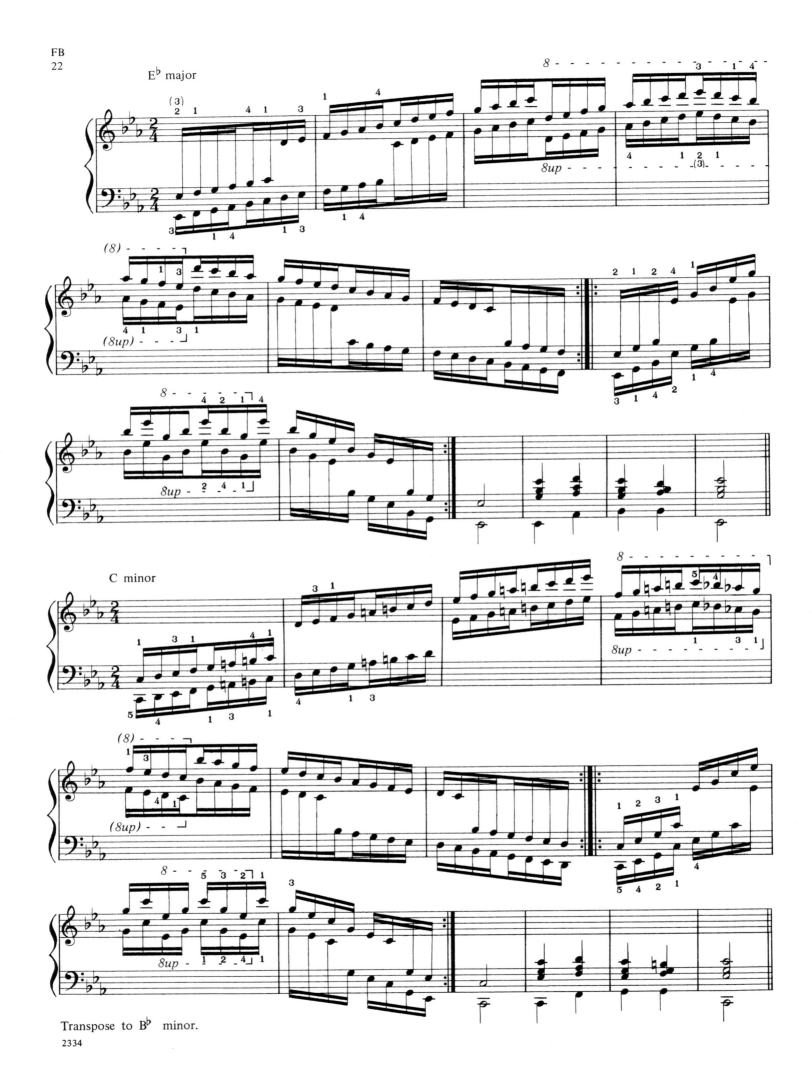

C minor

Transpose to B♭ minor.

Transpose down one-half step each day (F, E, E♭, D, and D♭ major).

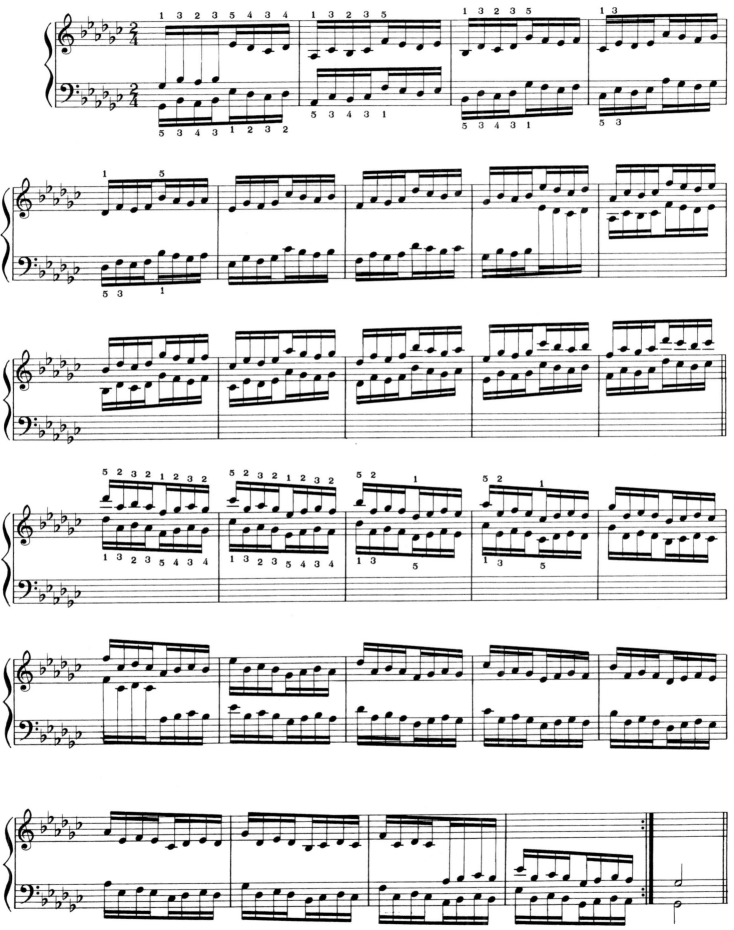

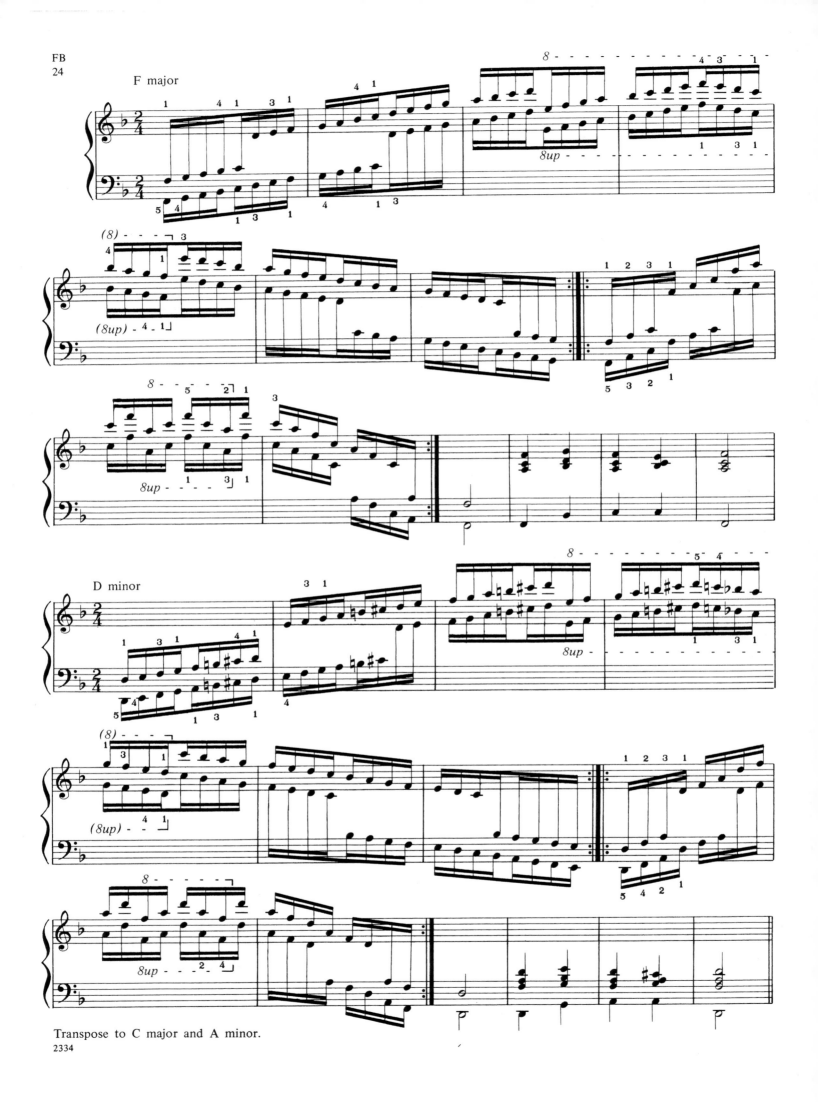

Transpose to C major and A minor.

Practice this as written, then reverse the direction and play it down the chromatic scale.
Work for clarity, eveness and speed.

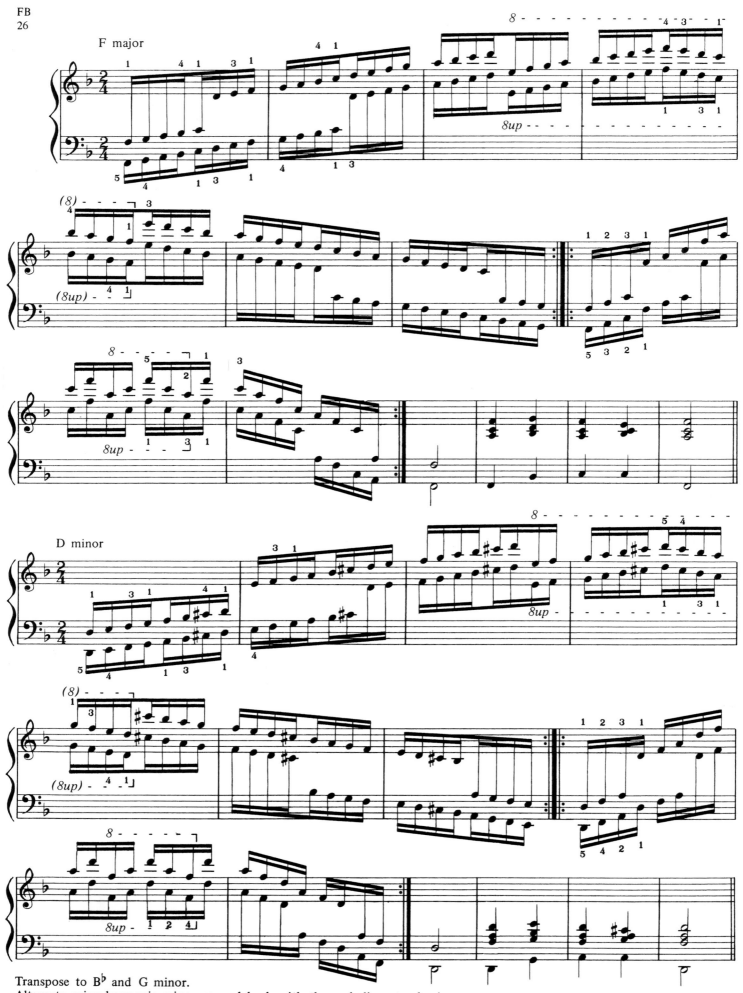

Transpose to B♭ and G minor.
Alternate using harmonic minor up and back with the melodic natural minor.

Transpose to the keys of G, D, A, E, B and F♯ major.

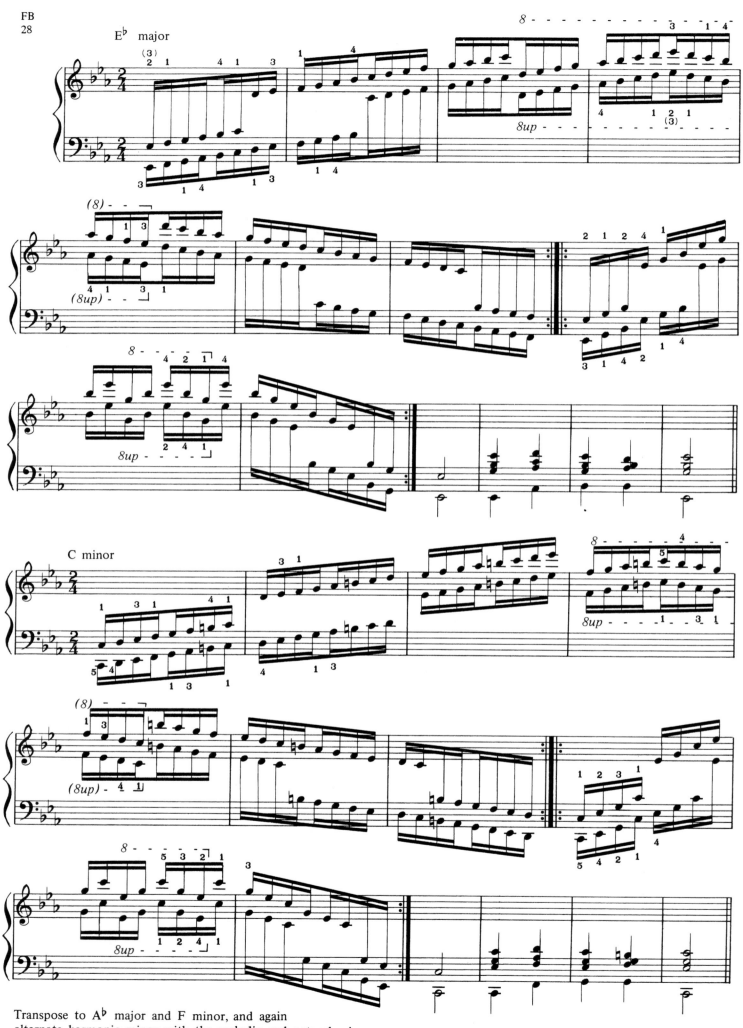

Transpose to A♭ major and F minor, and again
alternate harmonic minor with the melodic and natural minor.

2334

Transpose to the keys of F, B♭, E♭, A♭, D♭ and G♭ major.

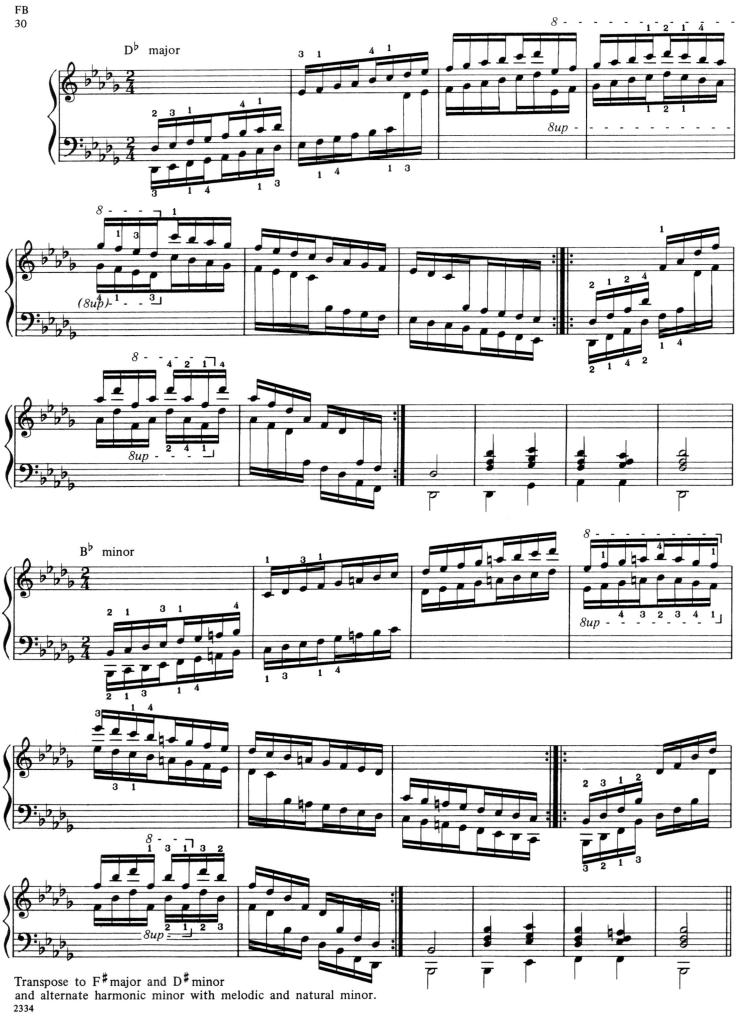

Transpose to F♯ major and D♯ minor
and alternate harmonic minor with melodic and natural minor.

2334

Feel the weight in the tips of the fingers and keep the knuckles firm.
Play both up and down the chromatic scale.

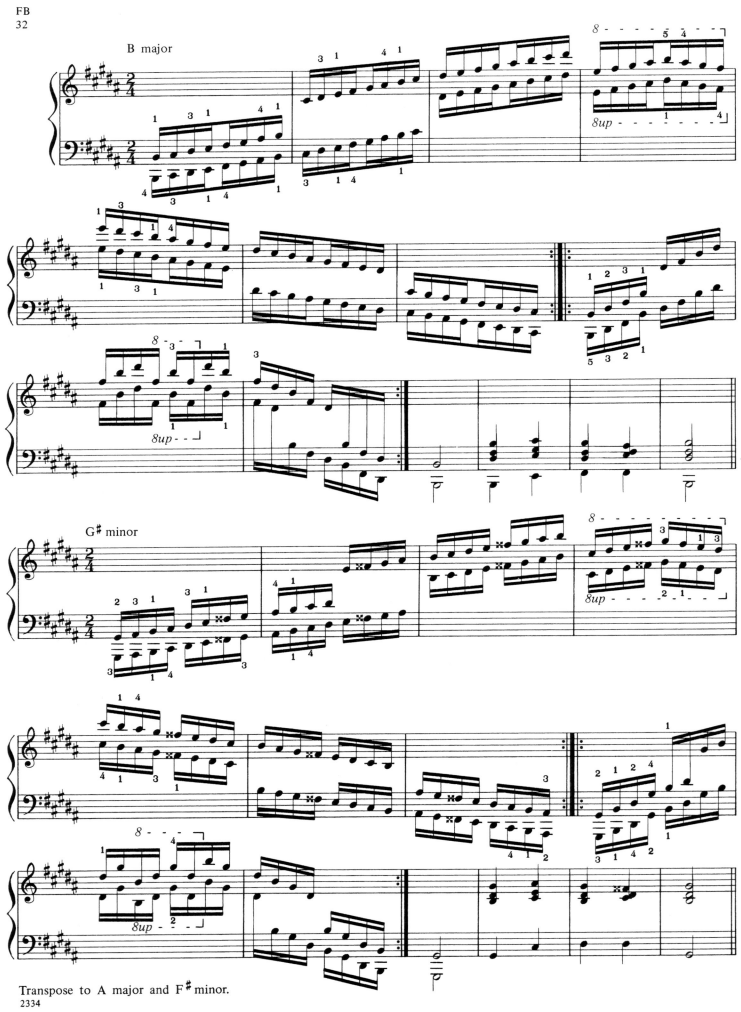

B major

G# minor

Transpose to A major and F# minor.

Transpose up by half steps to D♭, D, E♭, E, F and F♯ major.

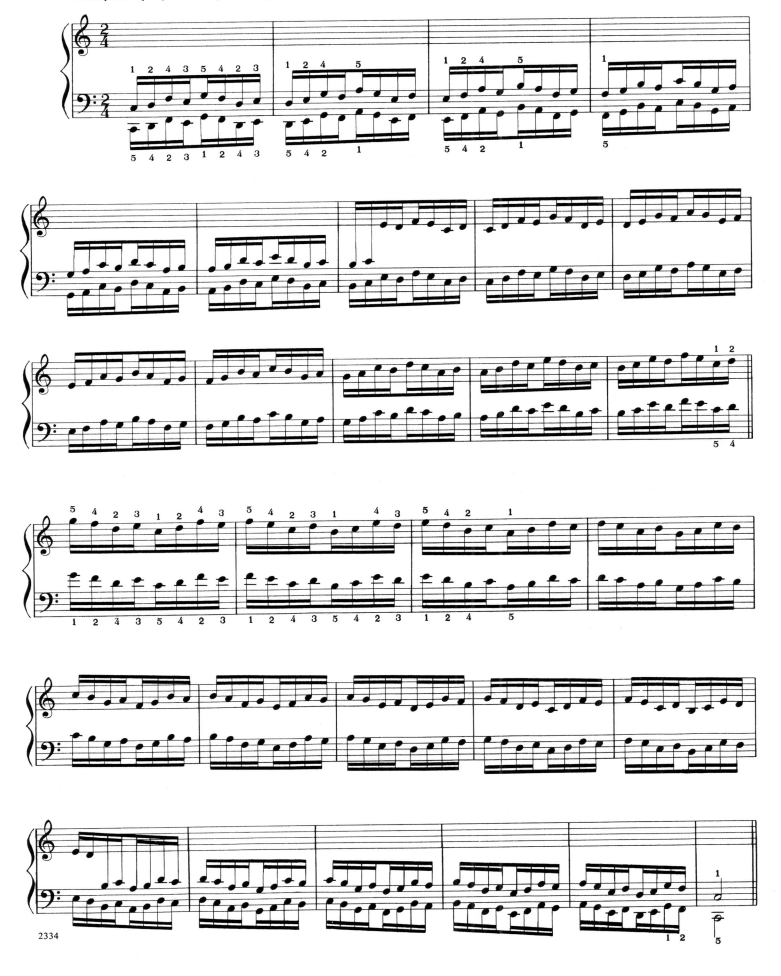

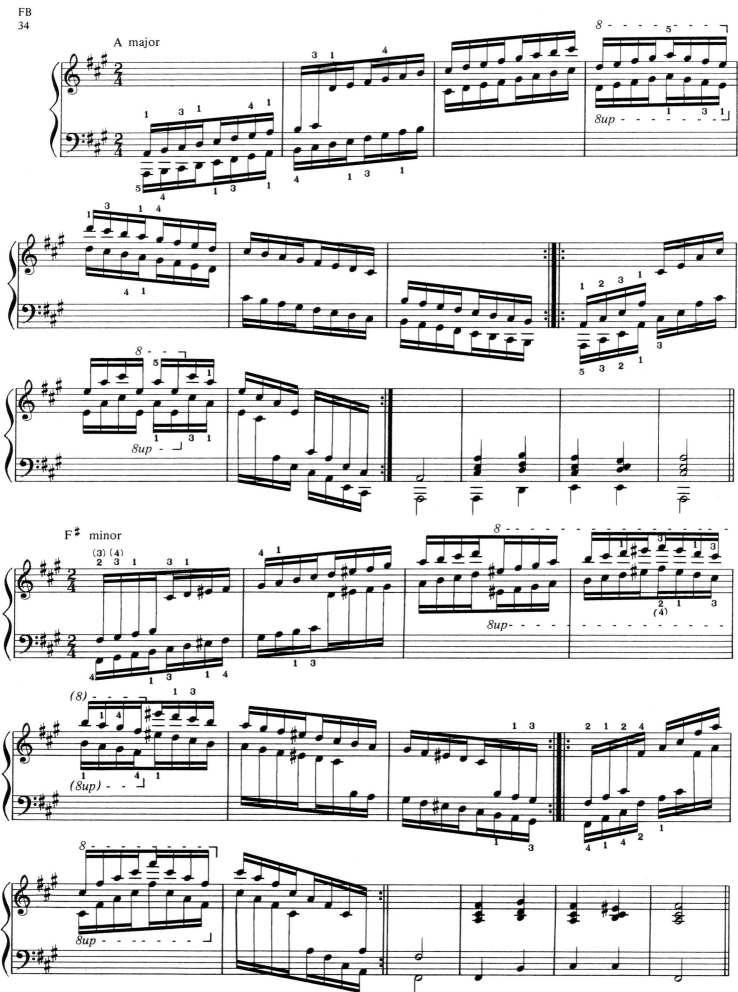

Transpose to D major and B minor (use both harmonic and melodic minors).

Transpose down by half steps to B, B♭, A, A♭, G and G♭ major.

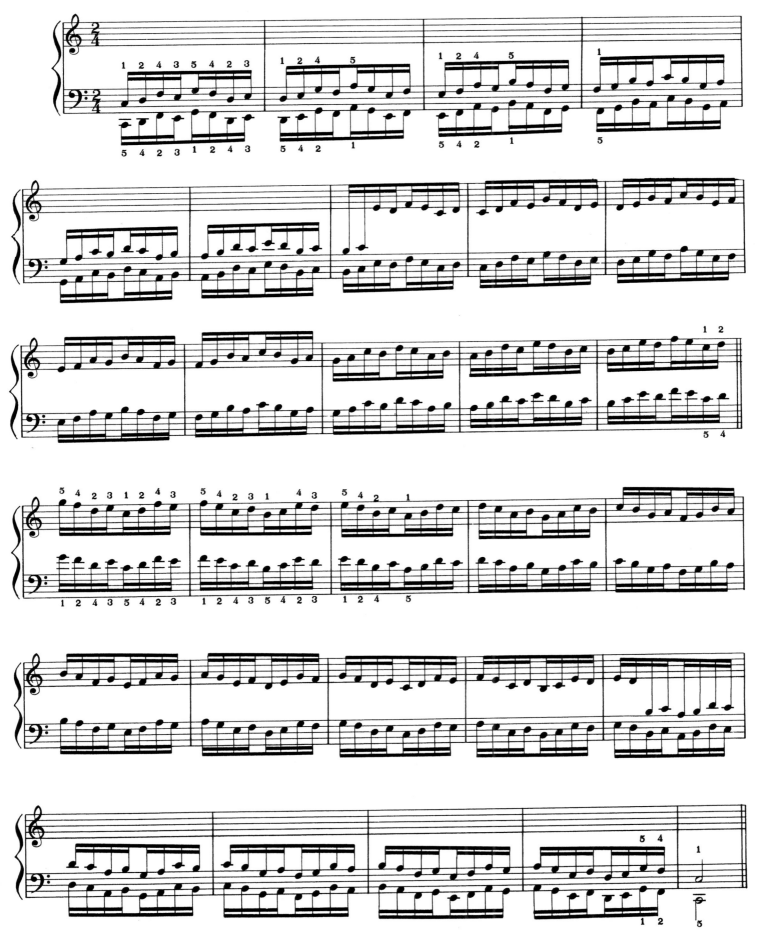

FB
36

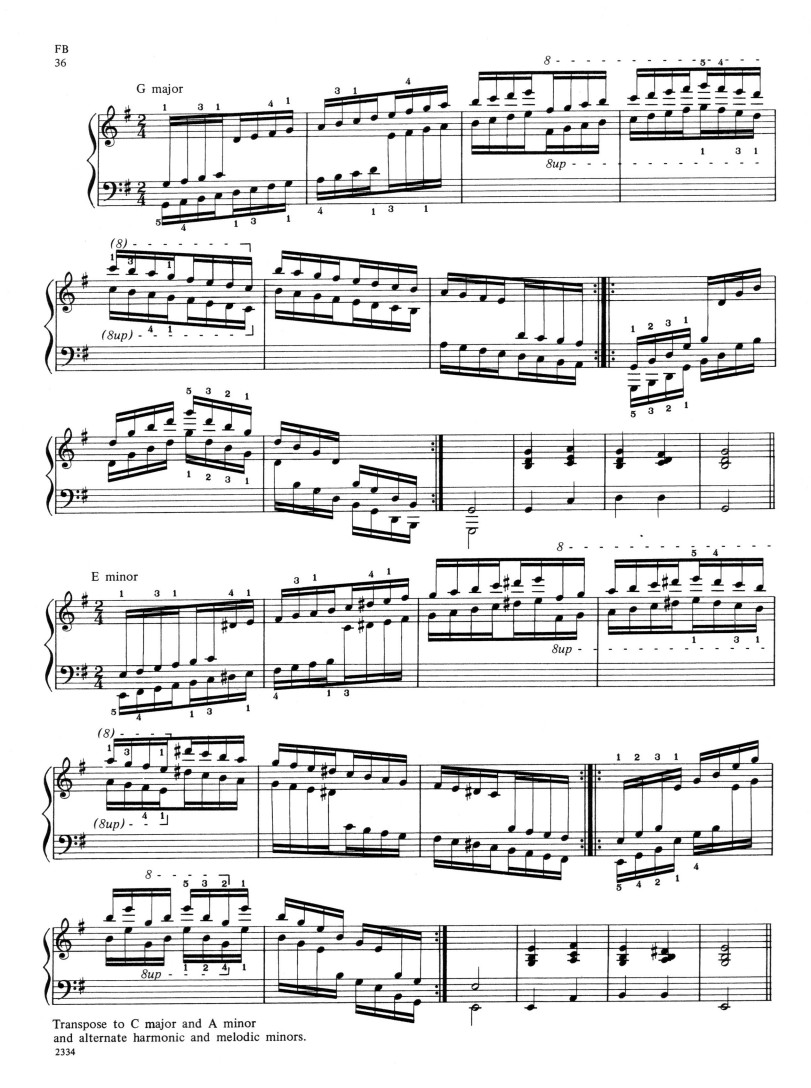

Transpose to C major and A minor
and alternate harmonic and melodic minors.

2334

Keep the hand quiet (no bouncing or wrist rotation), firm knuckles and lots of weight.

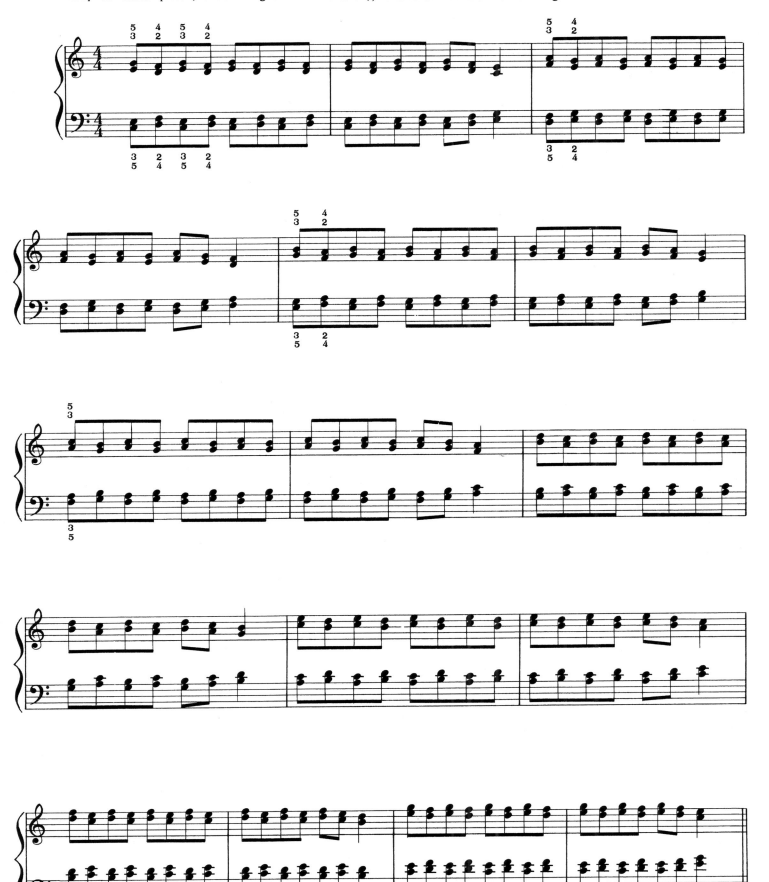

FB
38

C major

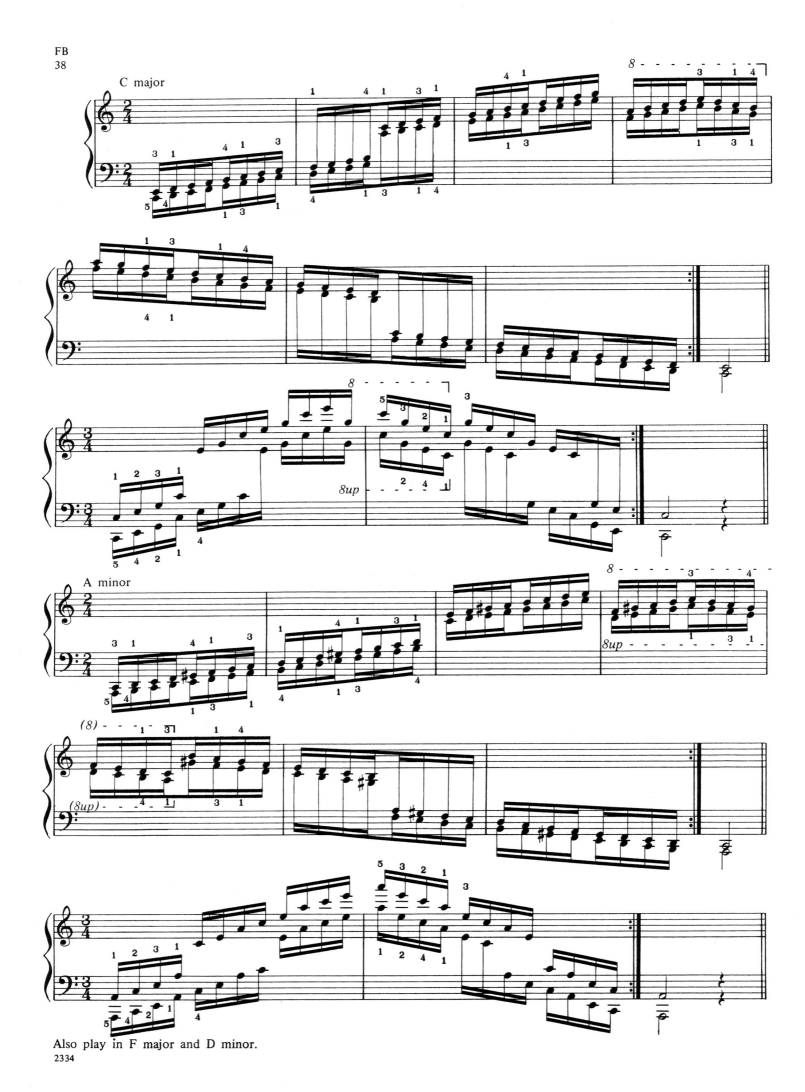

A minor

Also play in F major and D minor.
2334

Transpose up by half steps to D♭, D, E♭, E, F and F♯ major.

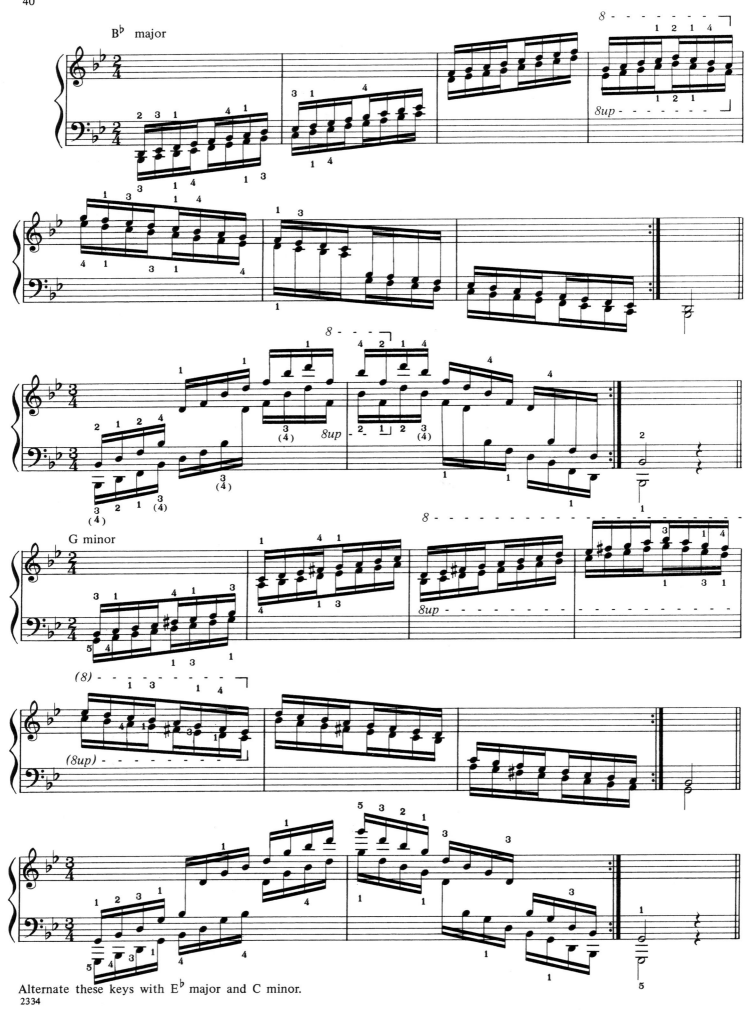

Alternate these keys with E♭ major and C minor.

Transpose down by half steps to B, B♭, A, A♭, G and G♭ major.

First, play as written, then on alternate days play in D♭ major and B♭ minor.

Work for clarity, accuracy and speed as you play first in this key
then in B, B♭, A, A♭, G and G♭ major.

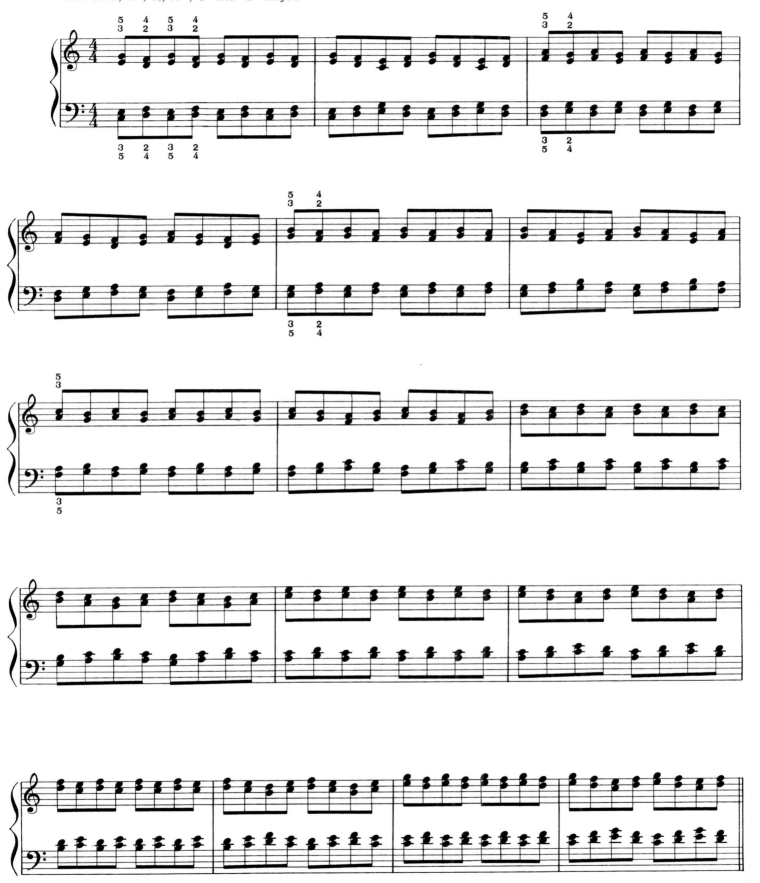

Also practice this in B major and G# minor.

Use a slight wrist rotation as you play this in the keys of D♭, D, E♭, E, and F major.

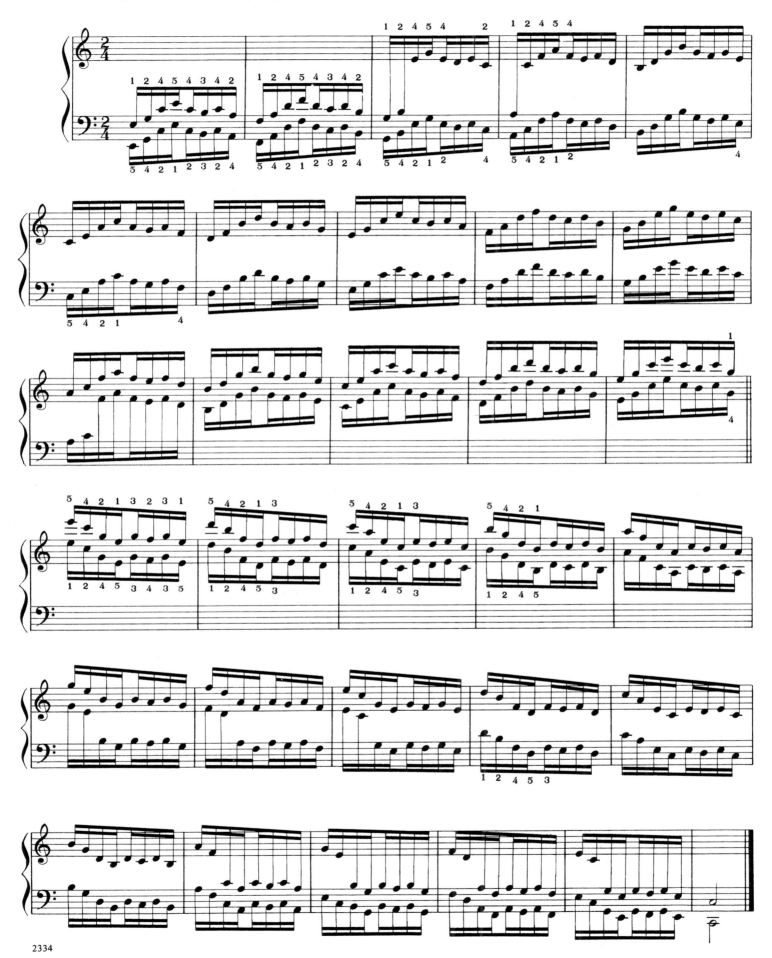

2334

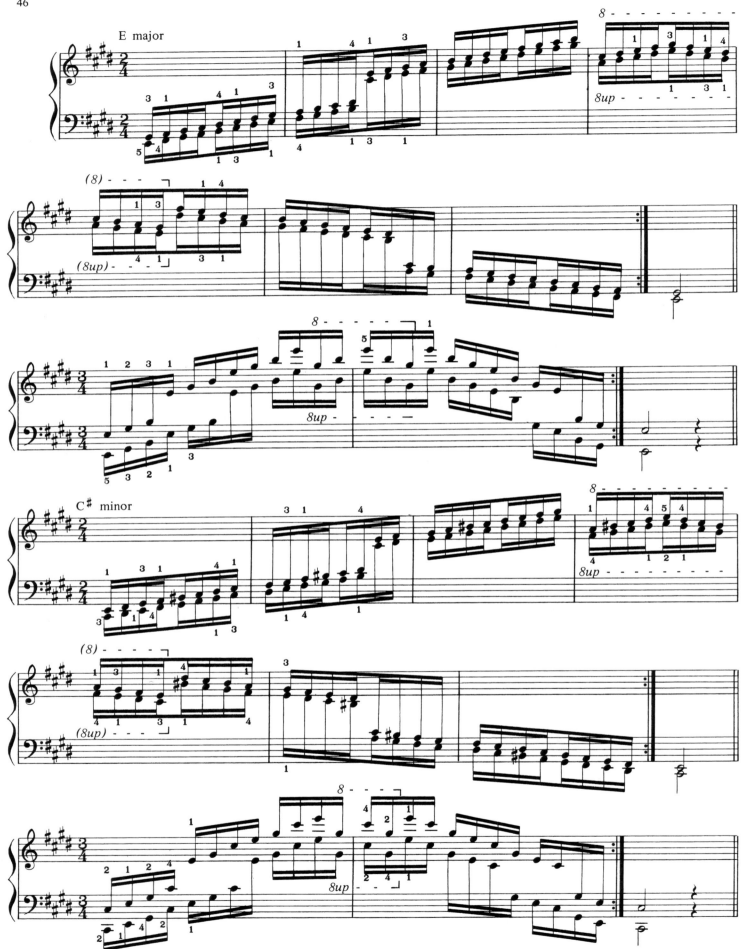

Transpose to A major and F♯ minor.

Again use a slight wrist rotation to get a very legato effect.
Practice in the keys of B, B♭, A, A♭, G and G♭ major.

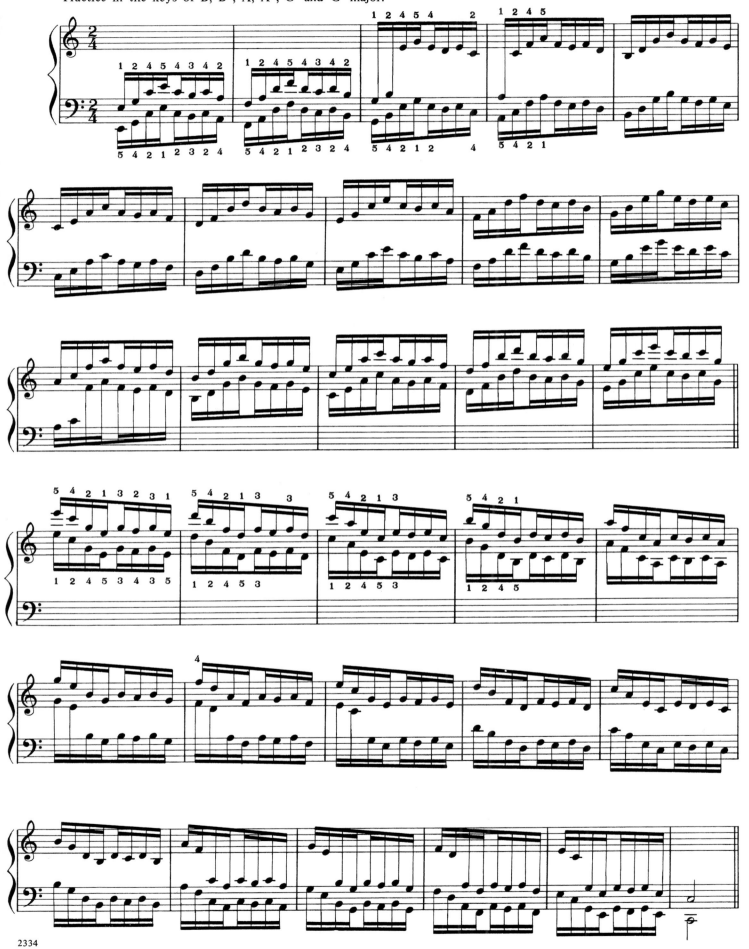

Transpose to G major and E minor, then review all major and minor keys.